Teaching Poetry

Teaching Poetry

A Handbook of Exercises for Large and Small Classes

Allan J. Gedalof

University of Western Ontario

W. W. Norton & Company, Inc. • New York • London

W. W. Norton & Company has been independent since its founding in 1923, when William Warder Norton and Mary D. Herter Norton first published lectures delivered at the People's Institute, the adult education division of New York City's Cooper Union. The Nortons soon expanded their program beyond the Institute, publishing books by celebrated academics from America and abroad. By mid-century, the two major pillars of Norton's publishing program—trade books and college texts—were firmly established. In the 1950s, the Norton family transferred control of the company to its employees, and today—with a staff of four hundred and a comparable number of trade, college, and professional titles published each year—W. W. Norton & Company stands as the largest and oldest publishing house owned wholly by its employees.

Dylan Thomas, "The Force That Through the Green Fuse Drives the Flower" from *The Poems of Dylan Thomas,* copyright © 1939 by New Directions Publishing Corp. Reprinted by permission of New Directions Publishing Corp.
William Carlos Williams, "This is Just to Say" from *Collected Poems: 1909-1939, Volume 1,* copyright © 1938 by New Directions Publishing Corp. Reprinted by permission of New Directions Publishing Corp.

The text of this book is composed in Adobe Garamond
with the display set in Bernhard Modern.
Book design by Chris Welch.
Composition by PennSet, Inc.

Manufacturing by Victor Graphics.
Production manager: Ben Reynolds.

Library of Congress Cataloging-in-Publication Data TK

ISBN 0-393-92582-X

W. W. Norton & Company, Inc., 500 Fifth Avenue, New York, N.Y. 10110–0017
www.wwnorton.com
W. W. Norton & Company Ltd., Castle House, 75/76 Wells Street,
London W1T 3QT

1 2 3 4 5 6 7 8 9 0

To my wife, Monique,
who inspires by example,
and my grandson, Misha,
who at ten months old loves poetry
and knows when to turn the pages.

*

Contents

*

Preface

This book is about ways to teach poetry and about what I think we're doing when we teach poetry. The two are necessarily interrelated, with the former driven by the latter. In what follows, I've embedded in the specific exercises, the how-to part of the book, elements of my own thoughts about and philosophy of teaching, in their latest and always provisional incarnation. I continue to be fascinated by both poetry and teaching and by the specific challenges involved when those two come together. If you're reading this, you probably share both the challenge and the fascination, and you probably share another problem endemic to teachers of poetry. We're teaching poetry because we have at least some degree of facility with it, probably a very high degree of facility that led us to the study and professing of literature in the first place.

You probably gained that facility intuitively or genetically, and to an unusual degree, a gift (but not a virtue; the virtue lies in how the gift is used) of great value conferred by whatever chance or process. It was no doubt honed on the strop of education, or at least not entirely blunted. You learned discipline-specific discourses of analysis, refined your understanding of language, sharpened your sensitivities to "the spider's touch, how exquisitely fine! / [That] Feels at each thread, and lives along the line," as Alexander Pope wrote in *An Essay on Man*. And regardless of where you are in your career, neophyte teaching assistant or grizzled veteran, you've probably forgotten what it cost you to get where you are, how much time and thought went into developing your relationship with literature in general and poetry in particular. Richard E. Goranson (formerly of the psychology department of York University) addresses this issue in his very useful study "A Paradox in Educational Communication" (1976), where he demonstrates that "after the solution to a problem is known, the problem itself appears to be inherently less difficult." Goranson suggests that we characteristically underestimate by a factor of between three and five the time and intellectual effort it takes to learn a concept and that this is transferred to the way we teach. The problem probably worsens with time, as in the story of the quite senior University of Toronto English professor who complained to his class, "I've been telling you this for twenty-five years and you still don't get it." Too often, we don't even know where our students are starting from, and we forget to slow down, to say the obvious, to give them some time to practise rather than just hear or see demonstrated the skills and knowledge we want them to acquire. To guard against contempt, born of familiarity, for the basic building blocks of the discipline, I regularly tell my teaching assistants and myself, "It's all news to them." It's useful to remind ourselves regularly that we're teaching students, a significant number of whom don't share our facility (or interest), and that we've forgotten or don't know what they need to learn and how long it takes to learn it.

The following exercises and suggestions are ways I've found of dealing with those problems and others, described below, that arise specifically in the teaching of poetry. They are driven by a desire to increase the pleasure students get from poetry, to somehow share the *jouissance* that lies beyond even understanding. While the primary group of people I have in mind to use this book are graduate teaching assistants and those early in their careers, I hope even long-time professors might find some small thing here of use.

Teaching Poetry

*

Introduction

For more than thirty years, teaching poetry has been in many ways the greatest challenge I've faced in the classroom. More specifically, it's not teaching *about* poetry that constitutes the challenge. I'm sure there are a million interesting, even enthralling ways to lecture on poetry and individual poems. An especially good lecturer might hold a class spellbound as she demonstrates both her sophisticated understanding of the meanings and affects of a poem and her extensive knowledge of the poem's various contexts—literary, historical, generic, theoretical, and so on. Under such circumstances, an inspired student might decide that he wants to do that also, wants to learn the steps that allow us to perform complex and deeply satisfying dances with the most demanding of partners: great poems.

At this point, the real challenges begin, largely because too often this is exactly the place we stop, when we have demonstrated our own interpretive skills and the conclusions to which they have led us. We may have asked our students some probing questions along the way, especially ones that prompt students towards our understanding of the text; we may even have discussed some aspects of the poem, but generally we do as humans typically do: we follow a line of little or least resistance, genuflect in the direction of the great twin gods Coverage and Expediency, ask quickly if students have any more questions, and move on to the next thing. If we stopped to think for a while, which we should do in what is supposed to be this most reflective of vocations, we might realize that we are asking students to acquire skills we rarely give them time to practise with our help and under our supervision. Even worse, we will at a number of points in the year evaluate and grade those students in their exercising of those skills, doing so under the tensest of situations, when marks are on the line and the biggest payoffs of reading great poetry well are quite out the window. If we want our students to do more than witness our demonstrations of the intellectual and sensual pleasures that come from poetry, and from hearing in the mind or the material ear poetry's sensual music, then we also have to provide them with an opportunity to practise what we preach under the eye and with the help of an expert coach. Given that we have to find our personal balances among various aspects of our teaching and that there is only so much class time, many of the exercises that follow, not unlike drills that actors or athletes might practise, can be done in a very few minutes, or have variations that can take up a whole class or a small part of it.

Reading poetry well is one of the great tests and rewards of the intellectually and linguistically adroit. Despite the best and most well-intentioned efforts of literature teachers through the ages, however, acquiring this facility (and felicity) has never been easy and has never happened throughout a population. The gifts of language are inequitably distributed. In our time, developing linguistic competence strikes far too many people as unimportant when wisdom may be just a double-click away. Huge things are at stake in the study of poetry, though, incalculable benefits that extend from the tiniest of pleasures through many and varied truths and ideas all the way to making us better human beings. To be more sensitive to others' language is to be more sensitive to others, to perhaps become more tolerant, understanding individuals who find great and deep joys in both language and life. It is to be alive to possibility and slow to judgment, to awaken intuition and marry it with reason. In "butterfly bones or: sonnet against sonnets," Margaret Avison suggests that poetry is "the thrill precision can effect"; reading poetry well, she insists, involves both a thrill and precision, passion and reason, something more than proving "strange truths" to "peering school-boys."

Over the years, I have had reasonable success in communicating to students my own passion for poetry and in explaining more or less convincingly the strange truths and joys I have found in a wide variety of poems. Some few already shared in those pleasures and found encouragement and a kind of personal vindication in those demonstrations: It may be a bit weird to be so invested in something as generally taken to be arcane as great poetry, but in the model of their teacher these students were finding someone whose weird or uncanny skill in deciphering strange truths could be seen as a kind of power, a productive authority even if only within the hothouse of the academy. A far greater number had already chosen a place in the pit or on the sidelines. They might cheer the performance, as they might marvel at the gifts of a talented actor or sports figure, but to climb up on the stage or down on the field was out of the question. To do so was to reveal, they feared, their own inabilities and clumsiness, to spit out rocks rather than Turkish Delight. Many of these students have determined that not to try is not to fail, a common enough mechanism of self-defence to avoid frustration and anxiety. But not to try is also not to succeed or grow.

Since it's best to have some sense of what the problem is if we're going to devise and try detailed remedies, over the years I've brought this subject up with students, teaching assistants, and secondary school, college, and university teachers both informally and in workshops and conference sessions. The litany has taken on a certain familiarity. At the secondary level, poetry has been largely or almost entirely eliminated from the curriculum. Its inclusion in any substantive manner requires a teacher of strong inclination, imagination, and will, one who chooses to teach poetry in the face of social, governmental, and institutional indifference and with students who, for the most part, have not yet acquired a language sophisticated and precise enough to appreciate or express the niceties of most discourses, let alone those of great literature. I suspect that even senior high school students who self-select to do advanced courses in English write more poetry for their personal writing folders than they read. A survey of first-year English students conducted by Professor Alan Somerset at the University of Western Ontario clearly revealed that apart from an exceptional few, most students had studied very little or no poetry, that what most had read was in almost every case quite contemporary (the most common answer of all was "I think we did a few poems by Atwood"), and that many had forgotten even the titles and authors of works they had covered only a few months earlier. Understand, I do not assign blame here. The roots of the problem run widely, finely, and deeply through our cultural landscape, and their analysis, inviting as that might be in another place, is out of place here. Instead, the question here is about damage control. Given what faces us, what can we do?

In short, then, and first, what do we face when students come to us in our first-year courses? First, we should begin with the assumption that it's all news to them, and important news too that we deliver without shame or apologies. There's no point in complaining about students' ignorance or the deficiencies of their previous education. If we care about what we're doing, and believe that what we're giving our students through teaching poetry is valuable, then we might as well proceed with passion, energy, and enthusiasm, confident that many of them will want to share in an experience that is so clearly a source of delight to us. I'm not suggesting that this is easy, or even that we are starting on neutral ground. Chances are that a good number of your students have had trouble keeping their love of learning alive in the face of their previous education. That's sad, because as Aristotle observed, a little nastily, in the *Poetics*, "to be learning something is the greatest of pleasures, not only to the philosopher but also to the rest of the mankind, however small their capacity for it."* Many arrive at university already jaded and with certain assumptions firmly in place. Because many designers of curricula have deemed poetry of minor utility or irrelevant, students may be unaware of or even hostile to the idea that poetry can add value and pleasure to their lives. Many believe that good poetry is difficult, and great poetry more difficult, so that when they encounter a poem with the golden stamp of greatness on it their first reactions involve anxiety, fear of inadequacy, or indifference. In a world increasingly focussed on the material worth of the things we learn, poetry becomes a harder and harder sell. Arriving at poetry's

*The Art of Poetry, trans. W. Hamilton Fyfe (Clarendon: Oxford, 1940), 9.

complex pleasures and rewards requires patience, skill, knowledge, and even wisdom, none of which is that mere double-click away. Many students can't see the point of interpretation and can't construe it as a game. They resent not having "fun." Some of them, not unusual in a species where xenophobia runs rampant, might even hate what they can't understand precisely because they can't understand it. Why, I've been asked repeatedly, can't these supposedly great writers just say what they mean in a clear and concrete way? Why do they have to make it so difficult and obscure? Aren't they just showing off?

You and I had better have some pretty good answers to those questions, or even better some good strategies for leading students to answer those questions themselves, because in many of our students we face full-blown *poesiphobia*, a more or less intense, more or less pathological fear and resulting hatred of poetry. How, then, do we get those students to experience the joys that precise language, diamond-eyed images, and the powerful play of intellect and emotion can bring?

The first and most general answer to that question lies behind the exercises that follow and underpins my teaching, yet is largely beyond the scope of this handbook. In brief, it is the ethos that I create in my classroom, the general tone, atmosphere, and attitude towards learning that I try to foster by displaying energy, enthusiasm, and passion for my subject and the pleasures I find within it, along with respect for, sensitivity towards, and interest in my students and their ideas. What happens in the classroom is not about me, but about my subject and my students' learning. What at any given moment interests me about a text is less important than what my students need to know so they can share in the pleasures of poetry. I have to find the difficult and shifting balance between making the text more available to students and getting out of the way so they can make discoveries, arrive at understandings, and use their own developing powers rather than merely marvelling at mine.

While we should spend a good deal of our teaching time interactively, we shouldn't dispense with lecturing entirely. We must weave the two together. Even as we demonstrate both the beauties and meanings of a piece of poetry and the pleasures we get from it, we must provide the benefits of our specialized knowledge and skills.

Even as we present contexts of various kinds (literary, historico-politico-socio-cultural, genetic, etc.), theoretical approaches, and so on, we must give students guided practise in the skills we hope they will develop. To become more perceptive, active, thoughtful readers, our students have to practise in class the very stuff of reading at a new level of linguistic- and self-consciousness, with us as coaches and prompters. Yet even when we try to teach more interactively, when we try to provoke discussion, we too often end up engaging in a series of one-to-one exchanges with a very few students, exchanges in which we remain the central authority and clearinghouse for all points made, or we ask questions that generate lists rather than discussion. We teach much more effectively when we centre texts and learners rather than ourselves, when we lead students to see that they can learn on their own and from one another. Perhaps oddly, our strong commitment to such methods doesn't make them easy to practise. Every course I teach becomes a race to get through the material I was so sure fit comfortably within the time frame of the course when I was designing it. Interactive teaching, making room for the students in the class, always takes more time than straight lecturing, always arrives at understandings and the appreciation of emotional and psychological effects more painstakingly and with more false turns. My impatience and sense of urgency often get in the way. Furthermore, running an interactive class requires the absolute presence of the instructor in the moment, attuned as fully as possible to the nuances in the cultural air, the sensitivities of individual students, the dynamics of the class, vagaries of expression, the good point struggling to be expressed in a language not yet ready to contain it. It's harder work than lecturing, where the instructor can remain in complete control and can even deliver a lecture on automatic pilot, the instructor's notes becoming the student's notes without even passing through the mind of either.

Such a monolithic or magisterial style is, I hope, becoming less common as it becomes less desirable. A growing body of theoretical works and a growing body of research into individual learning styles and into the different ways in which men and women learn are making it increasingly clear that if we don't need to revamp wholesale the way in which we conduct and participate in classes, we at least need to vary the ways in which we teach. To succeed with more than a small percentage of our students, to involve them in their own education, we need to extend our range of teacher behaviours.

Working as I do at the University of Western Ontario, a university whose heart is its business school, I take a somewhat entrepreneurial model. Students feel a greater sense of ownership of and responsibility for their own education when they have something invested in it, when they put something they value (beyond the fees they pay) on the line, when they have a stake in the success of their classes and the nature of their learning. To that end, I've been trying to decentre my classes (and extend them beyond class hours) by encouraging discussion and *teaching* among students. The first principle here is that not all learning has to go through the professor. The corollary to this is that the professor doesn't have to comment on or respond to every utterance by a student. Keeping these principles in mind helps head off the powerful temptation to intervene, to save time, to take the shortcut of control that leads to mere knowledge rather than taking the long and winding road to understanding and wisdom.

General Observations and Suggestions

Although some of the exercises below, particularly the more straightforward ones, may come across as strictures, their presentation has more to do with convenience than with my attitude. I am wary of the normative and would hate to have my own practises be seen in that way. In some cases, I've presented some exercises, whose success might be more difficult to imagine, in a more narrative form and have tried to record some of the experience of using these exercises.

I have never used all the exercises in a single course. With a few exceptions, I'll use any of them at most a few times during a course and most of them only once.

Some things work better with certain classes than others and with certain students than others.

Not all exercises will work for all instructors. Teaching is always in part a function of personality, and many will find that in ways large or small they have to adapt these methods to their own practise. Others may find them useful only as a springboard or spur to their own inventions or refinements. That should be more than enough.

When gauging the success of any exercise (or class, for that matter), consider this: If you're doing well, you are teaching or reaching, bringing about some change in, about 60 percent of your students, by my rough estimate. About 20 percent of your students are really smart and talented and can do the work pretty much on their own, or take a mere hint or suggestion and run with it. At the other end of the class, about 20 percent of the students are hard to reach for a variety of reasons. They may be any or some of: unmotivated, uninterested, unsure of why they're in the class at all, not talented in our discipline, just not smart enough, or depressed, anxious, or otherwise troubled. Aim for that middle 60 percent who can really benefit from your instruction.

Many of these exercises can be completed very quickly, some taking five minutes or less. They have their own intrinsic values, but also can be used to kick off a class and get the students' focus sharp and their thinking up to speed, to break up a dense lecture and move students from passive to active learning, to produce a little surge in learning near the end of a class, or in some cases even for a whole class.

Teaching poetry is work requiring patience and time. If we hope to have our students develop complex sensitivities, understandings, pleasures, and skills, we have to let them practise those very things in class rather than only testing them in essays and examinations.

The greatest incentive you can give to learning inside and outside your class is through the ethos—the joint force and full result of all of your behaviours and attitudes—that you create in your class. Think hard about the kind of class you want, that best suits you, your discipline, and your particular students. I hope that some of the exercises below will help you get there.

The pleasures of poetry are real and lasting. To teach others to better share in them is to walk with the angels.

A. Performance-Based Exercises

Exercise 1: The Five-Minute Reading: A Listening and First-Contact (Sight) Analysis Exercise

Years ago, I became rather frustrated with the student-led seminars I was using as a regular component of honours courses, where short papers were delivered by students and then commented on by the rest of the class (note that I'm not talking about seminar courses themselves, which I think are wonderful opportunities). These seminars were very uneven in quality and were too often painful for both the deliverer and the auditors, and although I stressed the importance and benefits of participation in this exercise, classes in which students were giving seminars were sparsely attended. Except in the cases of the most gifted and dedicated students, who were going to become involved and speak up in class anyway, student seminars no longer seemed like a productive way to use class time. Yet I still needed something that would give my students the opportunity to work on the various skills that doing those seminars were meant to develop in those giving them and hearing them. I wanted to have a class that was multivocal, have students take responsibility for their own learning, promote cooperative learning, develop research and analytical skills, improve written, oral, performance, and presentation skills, bring relevant supplementary material, selected by the students, into the course, and so on. I realized that some of those skills and aims were already being served, and served better, by other components of the course. What at first sight might seem like the most important elements of doing the seminar, the development of research, analytical, and writing skills in particular, were already being well-served by the essay component of the course, and by assigned passages. I decided to try a reading, listening, and analysis exercise in place of the seminars, since those are among the most fundamental and portable of skills and are ones students can use whether they go on to a career studying and teaching literature or not.

What I came up with, and have used regularly since, is a ten-minute exercise that begins as many classes as there are students in a course. The first five minutes is one student's reading, selected by the student from material not on the course prescription, relevant to the day's class. For the next five minutes, the other students respond aloud to anything they find interesting or germane about the material read, perhaps commenting on the form, structure, meaning, techniques, and devices of the piece, or on its relation to the work being discussed that day as well as to other material in the course. The reading can be other work by the author being considered, work in the same or a similar style or genre or on a similar theme or subject from the same or another period (students seem to especially enjoy finding connections between historical and contemporary materials), period reviews and responses to the work, and so on. I suggest material (letters, journals, essays, ballads, pamphlets, magazines) from the period in question as a useful source for readings, hoping that my students will dip into that rich pool of writing that surrounds and reflects the literature. I ban more or less current literary criticism, since the students will explore that material for their essays and I will be introducing some of that material in the class anyway. The readings prove uneven in quality, but they are less uneven than the seminars they replaced, students are less anxious about them, and they have no effect on attendance. In addition to developing the skills noted above, the exercise ensures that at least one student comes prepared to discuss the day's work.

Running the exercise

1. Since this is a graded exercise, you should put this in your course outline. Here's a version that I use: "5-MINUTE READINGS (10% of the final mark for the course): As per a schedule we will set during the first two weeks of the course, each student will, at the beginning of one class, do a five-minute reading of something relevant to the day's material, to be followed by a brief discussion of that material by the rest of the class. That material can come from within or without the period, and can be supplementary material from the author we are discussing or other authors who write in the same or a similar genre, style, form, or on a similar theme or subject. You can also select material from letters, journals, magazines and newspapers, ballads, songs, reviews, and responses contemporary with the work we are discussing, and so on. Remember that this is not a research seminar but a reading of supplementary material for the course, so the one body of material I don't want you to read from is books and articles of current literary criticism. If you're not sure of the appropriateness of something you've selected, or are having trouble knowing where to look or what to look for, I'll be glad to offer suggestions. If you're concerned about your performance of the reading, please feel free to consult with me also, and I will give you what help I can. You will be graded on, in descending order of importance, your selection of material, your presentation of it, and your contribution to the discussion that follows. You will also be expected to explain, in fifteen seconds or less, why you selected the piece."

2. I pass the sign-up sheet around class during the second week of the course, and a few times thereafter since not all students are always present. After that, I post the list on my office door, so that stragglers can sign up and amnesiacs check to see when they're on.

3. Early in the course, especially for the first few readings, expect to do a significant amount of the analysis that immediately follows the reading yourself. Once you have modelled how the exercise can work and what kinds of things students can respond to and talk about, gradually shift the burden to students. After the first two or three readings, move from your own direct responses to prompting responses from the class by asking questions, and after that, on good days, just sit back and listen, making only strategic interventions

when necessary or when something of unusual importance or utility is being neglected. As with many of the exercises that follow, students get better at this over time, which is all to the good since being able to analyse and respond to texts without the help of lectures is what they will do as readers, professional or amateur, for the rest of their lives, and learning how to do this kind of first-contact analysis well is like getting the keys to the treasure room.

Exercise 2: Memorized Readings or Performances of Poems

While I use the five-minute reading in honours courses, I do a simpler version in tutorials for first-year courses, where I have students choose short poems or passages from longer ones (usually about twenty to twenty-five lines, although I get a fair number of sonnets), memorize them, and then perform them at the beginning of the tutorial. What they read, in this case, does not have to be relevant to the day's material: the important thing is that they select something they like and that has meaning for them, and I ask them to explain briefly why they selected that particular piece. We do a schedule at the beginning of the year, just as for the five-minute readings above, and I allow a few minutes for the other students to respond to the piece. This quite simple exercise gets everyone to speak in class at some time and to know at least one poem and get comfortable with it; plus, it provides some training in sight analysis and practise in pubic speaking, introduces new material of the students' choice into the class, and acts as a kind of warm-up exercise to the tutorials in which there are readings.

Running the exercise
1. Have the students pick dates for their readings on a schedule you circulate.
2. Ask students to provide you with a copy of their reading one week in advance, so you can prepare an overhead slide (preferred for environmental reasons) or photocopies (which have the advantage of giving the class something to take away as a record of the experience) of the selection that can be followed while the student

reads/performs. Students hear better and understand more when they can also see the words.

3. The simplest way to run this exercise is to just have the student explain briefly why he has chosen the particular reading, and then have him do the reading. If the rest of the class doesn't start applauding spontaneously, you should. At this point, just move on to the rest of the day's business.

4. Alternatively, and this is my preference, you can spend a very short time discussing the piece that was read, calling for questions or comments from the students, and having a few ready yourself, which you can do because you had the piece a week in advance. You will probably have to do more of the responding yourself at the beginning of the year, to model ways of responding to the reading, but don't fall into the trap of continuing to do that because it's easier for both you and the students. As is always the case, if you want students to develop skills, you have to get them to practise those skills.

Exercise 3: Three Readers

3A. THREE READERS: A CASE STUDY

One of the happiest teaching experiences I've had was the first time I tried this exercise. I was teaching *Hamlet* to a very bright first-year class of 120 students and wanted to do three main things: to impress upon them the importance of performance as an act of interpretation, an act that generates highly particularized meanings that can lead to or affect a reading of a whole play; to get them to think about how characters put on performances within the play and even try to direct the play from within; and finally to discuss *Hamlet's* self-reflexive or metatextual elements and their particular appropriateness in that play. My general argument was that, from the play's outset, a number of characters struggle to get control of its direction: Claudius and Hamlet are obvious director figures, but Gertrude also tries to direct Hamlet's performance, the Ghost tries to direct or even script the action that follows his appearance, Polonius tries to direct, and so on. I hoped to show the class some of the complexity of what goes on in a specific performance of *Hamlet* by

showing how differences in the performance of a single speech by a
single character could have a far-reaching effect on the impact and
meaning of the whole play and perhaps even teach us something
about that character, about *Hamlet*, theatre, and performance in
general. Of course, I wanted to increase students' sensitivity to lan-
guage, to help them become more aware of their role in the produc-
tion of meaning and the relationship between understanding and
pleasure, and to thereby increase the range of pleasures and mean-
ings available to them. The students turned out to be very interested
in the whole process of how we negotiate meaning with a text,
especially a text that has the reverential status of a Shakespeare play
and that therefore doesn't just roll over and submit to any read-
ing it's given. This first-year class, and others since, asked some
very complex questions and offered some excellent ideas as they
grappled with major concerns in literary theory, incidentally provid-
ing the timely opportunity to introduce some of that material to the
class.

In the session before the one in which I planned to do this exer-
cise, I explained briefly that in the next class I was going to talk
about performance and metatheatre and asked for three volunteers
to read a speech by Claudius and three to read a speech by Ophelia.
I offered to do some coaching, as opposed to directing, should the
volunteers want it. On this first occasion, only one of the six, a
Claudius, wanted to rehearse the speech with me. That has proved
to be a pretty good rule of thumb for this exercise, including when
I've done it with nondramatic texts: about one in five asks for help
with the performance. I made the offer of help as part of my broad
aim to lower the risk for students who participate in class, especially
in large classes, by which I mean classes of fifty or more. The volun-
teers followed gender lines the first time I tried this exercise, so on
subsequent occasions when I was doing dramatic speeches I made
clear that gender lines could be crossed. I'll give you the two
speeches so you can think about them a little, and then I'll tell you
what happened.

Hamlet, *Act III, the end of Scene I*
This speech is delivered following Hamlet's exit after his "To be,
or not to be" soliloquy and his "Get thee to a nunn'ry," feigned-

madness scene with Ophelia. Claudius and Polonius, hidden, witness the scene.

OPHELIA: O, what a noble mind is here o'erthrown!
The courtier's, soldier's, scholar's, eye, tongue, sword,
Th' expectancy and rose of the fair state,
The glass of fashion and the mould of form,
Th' observ'd of all observers, quite quite down!   5
And I of ladies most deject and wretched,
That sucked the honey of his music vows,
Now see that noble and most sovereign reason
Like sweet bells jangled, out of time and harsh;
That unmatched form and feature of blown youth   10
Blasted with ecstasy. O, woe is me
T' have seen what I have seen, see what I see!

Although the stage directions are mute, Ophelia most likely exits at the end of this speech.

[*Enter* KING *and* POLONIUS (from concealment).]

KING: Love! His affections do not that way tend,
Nor what he spake, though it lacked form a little,
Was not like madness. There's something in his soul
O'er which his melancholy sits on brood,
And I do doubt the hatch and the disclose   5
Will be some danger; which to prevent,
I have in quick determination
Thus set it down: he shall with speed to England
For the demand of our neglected tribute.
Haply the seas and countries different,   10
With variable objects, shall expel
This something-settled matter in his heart
Whereon his brains still beating puts him thus
From fashion of himself. What think you on't?

As I write this, it's hard to resist going on about the many beauties and excellences of these passages, but that is exactly the impulse

I have to resist in class. Often, the understandings and truths we value most are the ones we come to ourselves, so we have to give our students a chance to do that without getting in the way too much.

What happened generally

On this first occasion, five of the six volunteers read very well, and the smiles of quite a few class members showed how much they enjoyed being read to by their peers. Perhaps they felt more involved because their representatives were up there: it could have been them, and they seemed to take a certain pride and satisfaction in the performances of their classmates. The discussion that followed confirmed that they had been attentive during the readings, and they showed a lot of goodwill toward those who had read. Although the quality of reading or performance has varied in subsequent uses of this exercise, those general responses of the class, namely investment and involvement, pleasure, attentiveness, and productive discussions, have remained constant.

What happened more specifically

The Claudiuses: Although the Claudius speech follows the Ophelia speech in the play, for reasons I no longer remember, I had the Claudiuses read first. (That decision turned out to be fortuitous because the biggest bang came from the Ophelia readings.) Two of the three read well, but the third wasn't entirely convincing. Interestingly, the class treated that inadequacy as an aspect of deliberate performance, as a take on Claudius, a kind of casting decision that made a particular meaning, rather than as a failure of the performer. This lesson emboldened me to use the exercise on subsequent occasions, since it revealed that students, through a combination of critical sophistication and kindness, could and would separate performance and performer. On the one or two times when that seemed not to be happening, I simply had to remind students of the importance of achieving that goal.

My three Claudiuses read very differently from one another, and the different effects of the performances on the class were in no small measure attributable to differences in the personalities of and tones adopted by the speakers. These connections led to a discussion of casting choices as critical readings of the text, and as having profound effects on our understanding not just of that character but of other characters and of the whole play.

The first reader gave us a kind of Victorian melodrama Claudius, who did everything but twirl his waxed mustachios. This sly, wheedling opportunist and schemer was the clear villain of the piece, and we eagerly awaited his nemesis. The class also noted this Claudius's clear propensity to assume that others thought as he did (later in the year, when we were talking about Milton's Satan while doing *Paradise Lost*, a student brought us back to this moment in the discussion by pointing out this similarity between Satan and Claudius as characters whose self-interest and self-absorption led them to think in particular ways; I was very happy!). Believing that others were plotters and dissemblers too, Claudius correctly suspected Hamlet's apparent madness, but (the students felt) incorrectly believed that Hamlet's love for Ophelia was also part of a scheme. This interpretation in turn led to questions about Claudius's relations with Gertrude, and then even to questions of whether Claudius's statement about Hamlet's feelings for Ophelia have nothing to do with what Claudius really thinks Hamlet feels but what Claudius thinks will have the greatest effect on Polonius, to whom he is speaking. Even this fairly predictable reading resulted in a very productive discussion.

The second Claudius read somewhat timidly, taking care with each word as if language did not come naturally, as if the speaker was in no way made for command or public office. He seemed more like a pettifogging bureaucrat, somewhat querulous because things were not quite going according to plan, and now he had to improvise. A student noted that even the phrase "in quick determination" was painstakingly enunciated, so that it seemed paradoxical or false. This Claudius displayed no "quick determination," according to another member of the class, who noted that when Claudius asked Polonius what he thought of the plan, the question was sincere, although when probed the student felt this was a question about efficacy rather than ethics. The performance also prompted questions about the casting and direction of performers and about how casting against the obvious grain could have very useful effects on an audience's understanding of a character or play.

The third Claudius was tall, dark, and handsome and read easily and powerfully in a commanding tone of voice. He looked a little piratical, wearing a kerchief on his head and a gold hoop in one ear; it was as if Claudius were being played by Errol Flynn or were doubling as an actor playing the ship's captain in Stoppard's *Rosencrantz and Guildenstern Are Dead* (which we were to do later in the course). This Claudius was so compelling that he complicated Hamlet enormously. Maybe, some students wondered, this brother of the king made a better king than Hamlet's dad ever did, and Gertrude's migration to his bed made sense, maybe Gertrude was even in the plot to kill her husband, maybe the play is Claudius's tragedy after all and it is his fall and not Hamlet's that brings chaos to the state. In the end, the class felt, rightly or wrongly, that this reading did too much violence to the play, a conclusion that led again to questions about casting decisions and direction and their role in the production of a performance's meaning and affect, and to a discussion of the limits of meaning. Can we, they asked, like Humpty Dumpty (my addition to the discussion; we can play too, but not too much), have things mean whatever we want them to mean: are we the masters, or are the words? This, of course, opened an industrial-sized can of worms and raised theoretical questions to which I would return for the rest of the year. I was delighted also that they were talking about a play not as monolithic printed text, but as something that changes with every performance and with every decision made in preparation for and during that performance. A great deal was coming to awareness and being discussed, and the students were doing it largely on their own.

The Ophelias: Here I got even luckier and saw things I had never noticed before, a development I happily acknowledged to the class. I can't acknowledge to students often enough that I'm still learning and finding new pleasures, even when revisiting familiar places, and that my students are very much parts of that process.

All three Ophelias read movingly but without the large variation in tone and delivery that we witnessed in the three renditions of the Claudius speech. Instead, each performer chose to hit hardest on a particular part of the speech, as several members of the class acutely observed. One of the Ophelias hit her most plaintive notes in the first part of the speech, which as class members pointed out is where Hamlet is most strongly cast in his public role as model prince. Students went on to consider *Hamlet* as a kind of political or state tragedy, a subject I would take up later in speaking about questions of succession in Shakespeare's plays and the relation between Elizabethan views of world order and the orderly functioning of the state and society. Another Ophelia found greatest pathos in lines 8–11, where members of the class felt that Hamlet in his more private roles, as young lover and promising thinker, was most on display. In this reading, they felt, we were seeing less of a grand state tragedy in the Greek tradition (we had already done *Oedipus Rex*) and something more modern, a more intimate tragedy. The third reader seemed more focussed on Ophelia than on Hamlet, and her performance stressed lines 6–7 and 11–12, those that deal directly with Ophelia's plight and that paint her as the most egregious victim of the tragedy.

"So what kind of tragedy is this, anyway?" one class member asked at this point, and here I moved the discussion, interspersed with bits of what I hope was timely lecturing, to the issues I described in my introduction to this exercise. As I tried to keep track of the subjects that were coming up that I wanted to say something more about later, I felt that I could teach the rest of the year on the basis of that one discussion. I've had that feeling often in running this exercise, and while it hasn't always been as productive as it was this first time, it has never let me down.

3B. Three Readers with Lyric Poetry and Other Texts

Although I first used this exercise with dramatic poetry, I have since used it mainly with other types of text: with lyric poetry, prose fiction and drama, and even with some nonfictional prose, with similar success. While the range of texts you can use this exercise with is enormous, some will work better than others. My classes and I have had a lot of fun with poems by or passages from Donne, Yeats, Behn, Shakespeare, Pope, Wordsworth, Browning (especially the dramatic monologues), Dickinson, and Auden, with lyrics from popular songs, and with prose by Woolf, Sterne, Austen, Swift (try three Gullivers one day, or the Modest Proposer), Defoe (three Molls, three Crusoes work really well), Fielding (the narrator in *Joseph Andrews or Tom Jones*), and Joyce.

All of these suggestions, however, come with some caveats concerning the texts, the performers, and text and performer in combination. Here, a little forethought can avert potential problems and perhaps lead to greater productivity. For instance, a text that seems ideal for this exercise in one way, Dylan Thomas's "Do Not Go Gentle into That Good Night," could be a minefield in certain classes. It's not hard to think of much more controversial poems and texts than the Thomas, and confronting those dangers may be exactly what you want to do in your class, but there are better ways of doing that than through this exercise (see Exercise 7, Quescussion, for one example). Depending on what you hope to achieve, some texts will lend themselves better to this exercise than others, and you should think that through in advance.

Think also about who will be doing the readings. Ask for volunteers rather than assigning this task to particular individuals or using this exercise as an assignment to the whole class in rotation. Students who self-select to read to the class generally do fairly well. Using students who don't volunteer—and individuals have all kinds of very good personal, cultural, and other reasons for refusing—is potentially embarrassing for everyone. You can, of course, ask for particular types of volunteers, like two women and a man, or all one gender, or whatever combination you think will be productive, and if you know the members of the class, you can select judiciously from among the volunteers.

Cross-gender readings can be very useful, if you want to talk about gender. Otherwise, you'll have to work hard to steer the discussion in other directions. Using this technique with works whose voices are already strongly masculine or feminine can be useful once, but presumably you need to cover other topics also. Of course, poems vary enormously in the degree to which their voices are gendered. At some level, poetry must always be within gender and gender within poetry just as poetry operates within and contains other kinds of conditions and discourses, but some voices aim for a middle or neutral ground. In my experience of using this exercise with poetry, texts with less obviously gendered voices provide some of the best opportunities.

Here, for example, is an account of using this exercise with a very short lyric.

This Is Just to Say

I have eaten
the plums
that were in
the icebox

and which   5
you were probably
saving
for breakfast

Forgive me
they were deicious   10
so sweet
and so cold

—William Carlos Williams, 1934

What happened

Because I've used this poem and Williams's "The Red Wheelbar-row" (which prompts overlapping responses) several times with this exercise, I can't keep entirely clear what happened when, so what follows is a conflation of things that have happened on those occa-sions. First, I'll describe some of the variations in the readings, and then I'll set out a catalogue of things that have arisen in the ensuing discussions.

The readings: Typically, the biggest variations in readings relate to timing, tone, and the emotional intensity of the delivery of either the whole poem or certain phrases or words. I always hope that my three readers explore three of the four fairly obvious possibilities for treating the breaks at the ends of lines and stanzas: emphasizing each line as separate by putting a marked pause at its end; reading through line endings and pausing at the end of stanzas; pausing ac-cording to general syntactical practise (pausing accordingly where they feel a particular punctuation mark might normally appear. Here, the most common pattern is to read as if there are periods at the ends of ines 8 and 9 and commas after 10 and 11); or reading straight through, since the poem has no overt punctuation. Almost all readers leave a space after the title, which receives special emphasis even though it is grammatically continuous with and of no more significance than what follows. When I've asked about this, by far the most frequent answer has been "Well, it's the title . . . ," with the "duh" or "dummy" implied. That response, of course, can lead to an interesting discussion about what titles mean, particularly in the cases of poems whose title is their first line.

Although I have no idea what order these choices have been made in and thus what is cause and what is effect or even if such a relationship exists, the pattern of pauses almost always relates to the emotional tone and intensity of the reading. While almost every student has spoken rather quietly, some even whispering the poem, for reasons I'll outline below, those who read straight through usually give the flattest readings, with the greatest emphasis on the title, while those who supply punctuation or read the poem as if it were prose tend to be the most histrionic and to hit hardest on the sensual experiences of the last three lines. The latter readers treat the poem as three sentences and generally deliver line 9, "Forgive me," with the greatest emotion. They treat the last three lines as either explanation for the speaker's action, addressed to the recipient of the note, or confession of a guilty pleasure, delivered as an aside to the class as if it was not a part of the poem/note.

Those who pause at the end of each line, or of each stanza, tend to fall in the middle of the emotional range, reading neither flatly nor histrionically. When classes or the readers are queried about these choices, both groups usually argue that the readings emphasize the writing of the note and the pauses reflect the way these thoughts occurred to its writer.

The discussions: The emotional intensity of a performance might not indicate the performer's relationship with, and understanding of, the poem. When asked why they had read the poem in the flat and continuous manner described above, students turn out to have made careful, intellectual decisions. Their reasons commonly include a respect for the words of the poem, which they argue can do their own work, a sense of the poem's quiet tone, and the desire to make palpable the sensation or the interiority of writing the note. Generally, classes quickly pick up on the reasons for whispering or delivering the poem very quietly: it's as if the writing on the page, or the act of writing, has a sonic dimension, and if the writing is too loud it will wake the note's recipient. This observation has led to very interesting discussions about the nature of the relationship between speaker and recipient, which is usually characterized as tender, considerate, and comfortable.

The most heightened dramatic readings, provided by those who insert conventional punctuation, usually suggest to the class a different understanding of that relationship, especially when someone else has read the poem flatly and quietly. When they emphasize "Forgive me," and particularly when they deliver the last three lines as an aside, students convey more distance, and some tension, guilt, fear, or anxiety, in the relationship.

Responses by classes to the two other common types of readings, pausing at line or stanza ends, are particularly interesting. Most often, students feel that those readings draw attention to the poem as poem, rather than to its human drama. They ask questions or offer opinions about why the poem might be arranged the way it is, why line and stanza breaks appear exactly where they do, and what the effects of these groupings are. They usually go on to speculate about the differences between poetry and prose and about how the spatial arrangement of a poem such as this one draws attention to the way in which every word, even the little, ordinary ones as in line 3, "that were in," seem to do extra work when arranged in this fashion. A discussion of the economy and compression of poetic language, and its corresponding demands on readers, always arises at this point.

Unless the question of the note's location has come up during the discussion, I ask students afterwards. The first answer is almost always "On the icebox/refrigerator," but students usually end up agreeing that it's on the kitchen table. They tend to argue that the note was written at night, after the recipient had gone to bed, even though some say the writer could just as well have arisen early, eaten the plums, and left the house before the recipient got up. Most students also feel that a man wrote the note to a woman, regardless of who reads it aloud. When pressed to explain this opinion, some fall back on their knowing the poem was written by a man, while others argue that men are more likely to eat something despite knowing that someone else is looking forward to eating it. Sometimes, these opinions have resulted in lively, even heated discussions of gender, essentialism, stereotypes, and so on, and the further realization that despite the almost universal assumption that the poem involves a heterosexual couple, it really could be about any two persons sharing a refrigerator. During this part of the discussion, students usually compare this poem to others that evoke a particular dramatic context, notably Donne's "A Valediction: Forbidding Mourning" and Robert Browning's dramatic monologues, especially "My Last Duchess" (choices that probably say as much about poems I teach as about anything else). Here again, discussions of good poetry as language working as hard as it can often arise, and students regularly observe how much more there is to this poem than they had previously seen. At this point, I usually summarize what we might have learned from the readings and the discussion in both specific and general terms, that is, about this poem, this type of poem, and poetry in general.

Running the exercise

1. At least a week before, explain the exercise. Get three volunteers, offering to coach if desired. Having two readers makes the exercise too much like a head-on contest, a kind of read-off, and you may not get sufficient variety in performance. With three readers, classes focus more on the text in performance and less on the performer. Also, as noted above, get volunteers rather than picking the readers.
2. Before the readings, explain the class's job: to listen fiercely to the performances as interpretive, and to particularly note differences and the implications of those differences. Make clear that listeners should focus on the meanings, effects, and affects that arise from each reading, and not on evaluating the reading as performance. They can also note where readings seem to correspond, and of course they can discuss what they might have done differently and why. Throughout, they should be asking themselves: "Why this reading, this tone, this stress, this pace, and so on, rather than any other?"
3. Have ALL readers read before discussing any of the readings, lest discussion preemptively alter performance. Thank them, reward their courage. In the case above, where we did the exercise twice, the three Claudiuses read and then we followed steps 4–7 below, and

then did the same for the Ophelia readers. It's better to do only one short dramatic speech or poem or passage per class, and expect to spend a whole class or a significant part of one on this exercise if you are going to unpack it. After all readers have finished, discuss the effects of each of the readings individually before moving on to compare them with one another. You may want to ask the readers to do their passage again, as much as possible like the first time, to refresh people's memory during the discussion.

If you don't want to devote a whole class to this exercise, you might just have three people read the same passage and leave it at that, for the other students to take from the performances what they will. If you go on . . .

4. Gather at least several responses before you intervene. Add new fuel to the discussion only when it seems to falter early on, before you think you've gathered enough material, BUT . . .

5. Don't be afraid to give people time to think between responses. You don't have to rush into every silence. At the same time, don't be afraid to prompt people to explore the implications of their observations, to ask leading questions.

6. You, or volunteers from the class, can record comments on the board or on overheads. This helps keep the discussion focussed and productive. It's useful to group those comments by reader and to have a separate area to record more general comments.

7. Unpack the exercise as you see fit. This could include some or all of the following: adding some comments of your own (tread lightly here; you don't want to do this in a way that diminishes what the students have achieved); summarizing the comments and what they tell about the particular poem or character or dramatic situation; linking what the class has done to wider concerns about the particular text, genre, or theory, or the reading experience. Finish by spelling out the payoff of the exercise in both particular and general terms.

Exercise 4: Negotiating a Group Reading

This is one of my favourite poetry exercises, and it has worked well when I've tried it with all sorts of groups, from first-year classes to honours classes to sessions on interactive methods in courses on university teaching, even when I have no English professors in the class. I've had a group of engineers, physicians, and scientists get excited about Dylan Thomas's "The Force That Through the Green Fuse Drives the Flower" and hotly debate the meanings of the word "fuse" in that title. I've had non–English specialists tell me that after participating in this exercise they bought a volume of Dylan Thomas poems or a poetry anthology and read poetry for the first time since secondary school. That, of course, has been enormously gratifying. Indeed, "The Force . . ." remains my favourite piece to use for this exercise, not least because the poem doesn't readily surrender its meaning, but I've also had success with pieces as diverse as the opening of *Paradise Lost* and William Carlos Williams's "The Red Wheelbarrow" and "This Is Just to Say." Those last two are good because they're so short, and using a very short piece helps contain an exercise that can easily take up a whole class if you try to do too long a passage. Remember that the general lessons of learning ways to work with and get pleasure from a poem are far more important than covering a broad range of the particular meanings of the piece, important as that component of our job might be.

Ostensibly, the exercise is about negotiating how we are to perform a poem, and the central, simple-seeming question I pose to the class is to tell me which words or syllables they would like to have stressed and which they would like to have unstressed. The Dylan Thomas poem works well because it doesn't have a regular metric pattern, and this exercise isn't about scansion, or accentual-syllabic metre. Rather, as I explain at the outset, it's about rhetorical metre, about how in performance we are to give the poem a particular spin. During the exercise, students catch on pretty quickly, or I point out to them, that every decision they make will determine meaning and affect, which they have a large role in producing. I tell them they have to perform a pas de deux with a text, give it the kiss of life, give it an attitude as well as a voice.

As with all of the exercises here, I'm trying to slow things down, to teach the general lesson that patience, close examination, and reflection are essential in the pursuit of poetry's pleasures, in this case by asking the class to think about every word and every syllable both for their own value and in relation to the other words that form the web of the poem. I'm also trying to give students a sense of their own agency, some confidence in their own skills and intuitions, and some realization of how much more joy they get from a piece when they closely engage with it.

Running the exercise

1. Select a poem or passage and put it on an overhead slide. A short piece is best, since whatever you use will take a fair bit of time. For instance, when I do the Dylan Thomas poem, I rarely get past the first stanza and usually put only that stanza on the overhead. To be prepared for a number of eventualities, however, I have in my folder fall-back overheads, one with the first two stanzas, one with the first three, in case we proceed beyond the first stanza, and one with the whole poem, to project at the end of the exercise. Use the largest possible typeface on the slide and leave room between the lines to record the class's decisions about what to stress and what to leave unstressed.

2. Put up the overhead, then explain to the class what they'll be doing, as set out in the introduction to this exercise. Here's the first stanza of the poem, so you have something specific to focus on as you think about how the exercise might work:

> The force that through the green fuse drives the flower
> Drives my green age; that blasts the roots of trees
> Is my destroyer.
> And I am dumb to tell the crooked rose
> My youth is bent by the same wintry fever.   5

3. Starting with the first word, do the passage word by word. No word is insignificant; choices have to be made even for the simplest indefinite article or pronoun. I always tell classes that if they aren't sure what to stress, they should exaggerate the differences between stressed and unstressed syllables, shouting out the stresses to emphasize their difference from the unstressed bits. I do that when I model their choices for them, as in "The **FORCE** that through the **GREEN FUSE DRIVES** the **FLOW**er," the most often preferred way to read the poem's opening, with the words in bold shouted out, the others almost whispered. Because this exercise centres on sound, I use this opportunity to talk about the central role of the aural in poetry. I

suggest to students that they read at home in front of a mirror and watch how the pronunciation of certain words and sounds contorts their faces. I ask them to attend carefully to those expressions as indicators of meaning and affect and give them an example by playing with the sounds of consonants: "l,l,l, m,m,m, n,n,n, are nice, comfortable, kissy-kissy-pushy-face sounds, while f,f,f, p,p,p, k,k,k, suggest something quite different." I further suggest that onomatopoeia is more prevalent than most realize, and offer them some words they may not have thought of in that way, usually including some for shock effect, such as "shit," which seems to me to reflect the actual process of defecation, especially if the word is elongated, and "piss," which works similarly. Every time we make a group decision, I record the decision on the overhead and reread the poem up to that point before going on to the next word. I use a nonpermanent marker for this exercise, because classes sometimes go back and change an earlier decision in the light of their growing understanding of the piece.

4. I often get split decisions for the word "through" in line 1 and the word "my" in line 2, and these different takes always spark good discussions. In such cases, I record both choices, putting the minority choice in parentheses, and I read the passage both ways to let students hear the implications of their choices. I point out that rarely if ever are there absolutely right ways to do rhetorical readings and that good justifications often can be made for alternate readings. Every time a preference is suggested as we work through the piece, I ask for a justification, for the reasoning behind the choice and for some sense of how that decision accords with the others we've made.

5. Have a good dictionary handy for two reasons: to look up pronunciation for polysyllabic words, and to provide a range of possible meanings for a word when a crux comes up. In this passage, the words "fuse" and "dumb" always provoke good discussions. When I work with a familiar text and can anticipate at least some of what will come up, I photocopy the relevant dictionary entries and put them on overheads, sometimes preparing entries from three dictionaries, to teach the class a valuable lesson and research skill all by itself.

6. For this exercise, I completely avoid formal scansion and don't give or ask for names to any metrical feet or patterns that might

emerge. There's enough to do without that, and although I don't back away from teaching scansion on other occasions, it just gets in the way when we're doing a rhetorical reading and so much is already going on.

7. When you've gotten as far as you're going, either because you've finished the selected passage or because class time is running out, read the passage as the class decided it should be read. If the discussion produced split decisions, give a majority reading and a minority one. Alternatively, you can have a volunteer read the piece, or you can have the whole class read aloud together. Most satisfying is having the class give a choral reading of the entire poem.

8. Leave a little time for students to comment on this exercise. It's often useful to have them bring to consciousness the general things they've learned and the skills they might have acquired. At this point, you can also use the one-minute paper in one of the ways described below, as a review, a diagnostic, and a reinforcement of the day's learning.

Exercise 5: Three Versions of Three Readings

This "exercise" consists of three variations on Three Readers and on Negotiatng a Group Reading. I give no specific example because these variations can be used with just about anything, including fictional and nonfictional prose. Giving a voice to writing, even nonfictional prose, even theory, is very instructive to students and can complicate, or at least trouble, their understandings of a text's authority and their ideas about authorship and authority.

Running the exercise

1A. Pick a short piece (sonnets are great, but any short poem or strong passage will do), and read it aloud three times consecutively. Read it neutrally the first time, aiming for increasing affect over the three readings. You could even go right over the top in the third reading, emoting like a melodrama or soap opera character, or like William Shatner.

OR

1B. Have a member of the class pick a short piece randomly, purely on the basis of length, from the anthology. Read it aloud, three times in a row, trying to get a better reading each time. This is the bravura version.

OR

1C. Either pick a poem or passage yourself or have the class pick one, and get a volunteer to read it cold. Then have the class give the reader notes, as a director would after a rehearsal or a performance of a play or scene. Have the student read the piece again in light of the comments received, and then repeat the process one more time.

2. I've unpacked this exercise in two different ways, depending on what I wanted to achieve with the particular class. One method centres on the poem, and the other on the process of reading a poem, although whichever way you choose will still contain large elements of the other.

2A. Process oriented: This works best with 1A or 1B above. Discuss with the class what happened over the course of the three readings, both to your or the student's performance and to their own intellectual and emotional responses to the poem. Ask as many questions as you can in the time you've assigned for the exercise. It's best to prepare a list of these, because it's often hard to come up with productive questions on the spot.

Among your questions (and remember to wait patiently for answers; you're probing quite complex and in some ways sensitive areas) might be:

- Did the students' psychological states change from the first to the last reading? In what way? Did listeners grow more or less attentive, more or less anxious, more or less pleased or bored? What accounted for those changes?
- At what point did students get something more from the reading, if that happened at all?
- What are they more conscious of now than they were before?
- What have they learned from this exercise that can apply to their own reading practises?

2B. Text oriented: This works well with all three of the variations above, but is especially effective with 1C, where students will have a large head start through having already had to make decisions about the performance, and thereby the meaning and affect, of the poem.

Here, the questions obviously focus on the text and what and how it means. Some of your questions could focus on:

- the role of voice and tone, and of other, more specific aural elements
- meaning, form, figurative language, other technical stuff
- what difference *hearing* a text makes
- who is in charge of meaning

2C. Some combination of 2A and 2B (which often just seems to happen anyway): Regardless of which way you do this exercise, you might learn even more than the students do. If you take care to be totally present at your teaching, to avoid one of the big pitfalls of familiarity and habituation, going on automatic pilot, this learning can be one of the great joys of the classroom. Among what you can learn during this and many of the other interactive exercises here is how your students read, both in performance and as a set of practises, and how you read (although in the discipline today you've probably been thinking about that a lot already, and that's a good thing), and the differences between your own practises and those of your students. The things you learn become the springboard into the bottomless pool of pedagogic possibilities. The good teacher always tries to do it better next time, to make different mistakes, and to modify her teaching to suit her evolving understanding of her subject, herself, and the group of individuals she is teaching. In teaching, as in other parts of life, often the best we can hope for is to make different mistakes next time: "Try. Fail. Try again. Fail Better," as Samuel Beckett puts it. That wonderfully slippery idea, to "fail better," can give us both a certain leeway as teachers, since we know we can never get it perfectly right, and a certain challenge, as we can always get it better. In fact, the variations on Three Readings have come about, as have most of the exercises and their variations in this handbook, as a result of this broad approach to teaching.

Exercise 6: Scansion Exercises

Teaching poetry poses special problems; teaching scansion compounds them. Sometimes, the mere mention of the word *scansion* can cause eyes to glaze over and brains to shut down. Even some graduate teaching assistants react with fear or confess that they never really grasped scansion. We might ask ourselves, as I have done, why we bother at all when even those with a gift for literature have found it possible to succeed without being able to scan poetry well. Even the best students seem to memorize the names of a few types of metrical feet for a test and forget them as soon as the test is over. Despite all of that and more, I still believe there is great value in heightening students' sensitivity to and awareness of the rhythms that are so central to poetry and to life itself, and the study of scansion is a way of bringing those rhythms to consciousness and of increasing poetry's available pleasures. Here are a few techniques I've had some success with in achieving those ends.

6A. USING MUSIC TO TEACH THE DISTINCTION BETWEEN ACCENTUAL-SYLLABIC AND RHETORICAL METRES

Some of the problems with teaching scansion begin with the difference between these two ways of marking up a passage. Many students cannot see or hear the underlying metre of a passage simply because that underlying metre is not apparent when they or their instructor reads the passage in a more or less dramatic and interpretive fashion. That every reading *is* a reading gets in the way as we introduce expressive metrical shifts to reflect our own understandings or choices in meanings and affects. Getting students first to understand and then to hear how these two types of metre play off one another is difficult. I have had some success, however, in using a musical analogy and example. I liken poetry printed on the page to a piece of sheet music: it is written in a particular time signature, which is its accentual-syllabic metre, but the basic rhythm signalled by the time signature is varied—notes given more or less force, stretched or shortened, given emotional colours—when the piece is played by a skilled performer. The sheet music is potential, to be given a particular reality by the performer, just as a poem is by a reader. To illustrate the point and take it further, I then play two very different performances of the same piece of music. I often use Bruce Cockburn's "Lovers in a Dangerous Time," first performed by Cockburn and then covered by Barenaked Ladies. I've used some jazz tunes also (the Keith Jarrett Trio, for example, covering Miles Davis, or DJ Krush doing Miles). Once students "get" the analogy, I take it a step further by considering the format of a rock band or jazz group. I compare the rhythm section, drums and bass, to accentual-syllabic metre, in that each sets up the basic and underlying rhythm (read *poetic metre*), with and against which the lead instrument and lead vocalist can play (corresponding to the *rhetorical metre* of a piece). At this point, I scan a line of poetry (or two, but not more) both ways. Opening lines of Shakespeare sonnets work very well here. Students know that "Let me not to the marriage of true minds," "That time of year thou mayst in me behold," "My mistress' eyes are nothing like the sun," and so on should be and generally are in iambic pentameter because they are from sonnets, but when they read them aloud and stress the differences between accented and unaccented syllables, they recognize how bad or wrong the lines sound. When they read them rhetorically, they learn how many variations exist and how expressive and intrepretive those variations can be.

6B. Scan Your Name

This exercise had a curious start. When reading out the names on class lists at the beginning of courses, I would learn the correct pronunciation of each student's name and record that pronunciation phonetically where necessary, marking light and heavy stresses. Growing up with a name like Gedalof makes you sensitive to such niceties. Quite naturally, I began to see names as metrical feet. My name, Allan Gedalof, becomes Trochee Dactyl, which makes me sound quick and alert. One thing led to another, as it usually does, and Scan Your Name became an exercise I do very early in my introduction to scansion. I put on the board the common metrical feet (iambic, trochaic, spondaic, pyrrhic, dactylic, and anapestic) and ask students to scan their names. Then we go around the class and everybody announces their own name and its scanned version. You'll find an awful lot of Trochee Trochees in your class, but you'll also find some excellent opportunities with the more interesting-sounding names to discuss the niceties of scansion. Everybody learns and remembers at least one metrical foot, hears everybody in the class say their names, and paradoxically, while they identify themselves as individuals by naming themselves, scanning their names aloud also lets them end up with a lot of new relatives in their alternate identities as metrical beings.

6C. EXAGGERATION

When working on scansion, one of your greatest aids is exaggeration of the difference between stressed and unstressed syllables. Get the students to try aloud the various possibilities, both for polysyllabic words and for lines or parts of lines. Their ears will tell them a great deal, and they will learn to trust their intuitions, which are so often the foundations of understandings. You can also get the students to beat out on their desktops the rhythm of the lines they have scanned. Like exaggerating stresses when reading (a technique I also use in the cumulative reading, described below), this leads to a few raucous moments in the classroom. Pretty much everyone gets involved, a little pent-up energy is released, and you and the class experience one of poetry's most fundamental and pleasing qualities: its visceral, primal power. A group reading aloud together taps into the formidable power of choirs.

6D. NURSERY RHYMES

Somewhat similarly, when introducing scansion I sometimes use nursery rhymes as examples, combined with exaggerated readings by the class. Nursery rhymes offer productive examples because they have such strong and varied metres, rhythms, and rhyme schemes, the struggle towards meaning isn't usually an issue, and their familiarity assures a certain comfort level in the students (although I'm quick to acknowledge that a degree of discomfort is sometimes productive). Furthermore, this exercise will let students recapture for a regenerating and perhaps lasting moment the pleasures they found in rhythm and sound even as language was putting down its first roots.

B. Question-and Discussion-Based Exercises

Exercise 7: Quescussion

One of the most interesting and productive ways to help students move beyond their initial fears of and anxieties about poetry is the technique developed specifically for the discussion of poetry by University of Saskatchewan English professor Paul Bidwell. He coined the name *quescussion*, to signal a form of discussion conducted through questions. While quescussion can be used in a variety of ways, some of which I will briefly describe below, for our purposes it's best to start with the way Paul Bidwell has used it in teaching poetry. It's rules are quite simple:

1. Everything must be put in the form of a question; no statements are allowed.
2. Participants must wait until X (where X = 2, 3, or 4 depending on class size) intervening speakers have asked their questions before they can speak again. This delay prevents direct confrontations between two speakers where the issues are contentious.
3. No disguised statements, such as ones beginning with "Isn't it true that . . ."
4. The exercise is self-policing. The class should shout "Statement!" when someone makes one. This is usually fun.
5. Sometimes, it's useful to add a fifth rule governing nasty or ad hominem questions, such as "Is everyone who is anti–gun control, like my classmate over there, also a war-mongering, nose-picking, neo-Nazi cretin?" Typically, these turn out to be thinly veiled statements and are inadmissible on those grounds too. This rule is often unnecessary, but will come into play if the subjects discussed are ones that people might have strong feelings about, such as hot-button issues in politics, gender, race, abortion, euthanasia, religion, or hockey.

When Professor Bidwell first used quescussion, he would explain the rules and present the class with a poem on which he had not lectured. He would tape record and later transcribe the quescussion and bring copies of the transcript to a subsequent class, where the transcript would act as a road map for a further discussion of the poem. The benefits of using such a form of discussion are myriad. Ones that have struck me with a particular force are:

- Students get in the habit of approaching poetry by asking themselves discrete questions about specific parts or aspects of it, which they are not in the habit of doing. Instead, they usually have a crisis of meaning, panicking in the face of the whole poem at once, as if they had to eat a multicourse meal in one bite. Being able to approach a complex issue by finding a variety of points of attack, to ask a series of productive questions about it, is among the most fundamental of problem-solving skills and is generally underdeveloped. The study of poetry is a wonderful proving ground for this universally portable skill.
- Students not only learn the general skills of questioning, but acquire a large set of questions they can use when first reading a poem or other text.
- What's more, the questions are those of peers who share similar experiences and concerns. Our students are just like other humans in finding it reassuring to discover that others share their perplexities or understandings. Knowing that can lessen anxiety about reading, which can free more of the mind to think about and enjoy the poem.
- Students set the agenda, take a measure of control over and responsibility for the nature and direction of their learning. There's less "feed me" and more "I wonder what that tastes like."
- For instructors, the exercise always contains an element of the diagnostic. You may feel you need to say certain things about your subject, quite rightly, but your students need to learn certain things too. Quescussion, like most of the exercises here, allows you to learn what some of those things are. As Professor Bidwell uses this exercise, it directs the agenda for at least part of the next class.
- Students will try out ideas they would hesitate to express under other circumstances. Risk for students offering interpretations or readings is significantly lowered because everything, being in the form of a question, is about the possible or provisional. I often

point out to students that all readings are provisional anyway, and change with time, culture, and a host of other variables including changes in the reader and in the meaning of language.

- One of the impressive things about this exercise is how quickly it climbs the scale of cognitive functions in a typical taxonomy of higher-order mental skills, into the upper reaches where skills including synthesis, analysis, and evaluation reside. Quescussion quickly encourages quite difficult questions.
- Students and texts take centre stage, while the instructor's role should, ideally, be restricted to identifying the next questioner.
- Funny stuff happens. Not only is that good in itself, but it reinforces the association among learning, poetry, and pleasure.

Running the exercise

1. Give a short explanation of how a quescussion is conducted.
2. Present the text for discussion. If the text has not been pre-assigned for reading, give students a few minutes to read it. Even if it has been previously assigned, it's a good idea to let them read it again (or for the first time for some of them), or have a member of the class read it aloud. Try not to do it yourself, since your reading will do too much of the preliminary work of interpretation. I like to have the text up on an overhead, so that it always forms a focus for the quescussion.
3. Run the quescussion, the length of which will vary with the task that has been set, but which will rarely last beyond fifteen minutes and is more often in the five- to ten-minute range. It's instructive for both you and the class to see how much can actually be done in a few minutes. Classes have to learn how to do quescussion well, so don't despair if the results are short of spectacular for the first time through. Silences between questions are normal, even after the first time. Don't worry: they're thinking hard, and silence can be very productive.

An Aside on Silences: Typically, we fear silence in the classroom because it seems to signify a failure of social or intellectual productivity. We fill with unproductive noises, ums and ers, even the slightest of voids, and for the most part we leave no more than two or three seconds between the time we ask a question and when we despair of getting an answer and give it ourselves. Consider what has to take place in a student's mind, consciously or unconsciously, after being asked even a relatively simple question. It might go like this: Process the question—Am I willing to make the effort?—Do I know the answer?—Search for it—Find it—Do I know it or enough of it with enough confidence in its value to risk offering it to the class? (The bigger the class, generally the higher the safety factor has to be)—Formulate the answer—Put hand up. I'm not suggesting this is an actual sequence, since a number of these decisions and searches probably take place at the same time, but it might represent how many kinds of mental activity take place within that silence. I have schooled myself to wait seven seconds after asking a question before doing anything about the silence, and then I'm much more likely to restate the question or ask what the problem is than to answer the question myself. Seven seconds is often long enough to get to the class member who is most uncomfortable with silence and who will often preface his answer with "I know this is wrong, but . . ." Perhaps such students are just really nice people who don't like to see you hung out there to dry, but it's just as likely that they're made so anxious by the silence that they'd rather take a wild guess than have it continue. This, of course, almost always leads to further participation.

4. If the questions peter out (just who was this Peter, and what did he do to deserve this?) before you feel that you've gathered enough material, this is the time to intervene with a strategic prompt, preferably one that will open up a neglected line of questioning and reenergize the quescussion. You would do well to have a few of these planned in advance, because as some of your students are finding out and a lot of teachers already know, productive questions are often harder to generate than good answers.

5. Always congratulate and thank the class for their work. Don't immediately give them a list of the things they left out. If you do so, they'll think that the exercise was a test they didn't do well on, or wish you'd just delivered your complete list in the first place. In any event, they'll be less likely to participate enthusiastically the next time. If you want to add to what the students have provided, you can do so during the unpacking of the exercise while you discuss their questions.

Unpacking

How you use this exercise can really vary, from doing nothing to doing a great deal.

- If you choose to do nothing, and sometimes that will be the right thing to do, you have at least introduced your class to a range of questions on this subject that will have them thinking deeply about the text, and many of the questions will be useful to them when they apply them to other texts and problems.
- If you want to address some or all of these questions, you can follow Professor Bidwell's practise, tape record or videotape the quescussion, transcribe all the questions, and present them to the class as the focus for future discussion.
- Alternatively, you or your designate can record the questions on the board or overhead, grouping them if desired, and use them as a springboard to a traditional type of discussion or lecture that can follow immediately upon the quescussion. This has become my favourite way of using this exercise. I try to think of how I will group the responses in advance of the exercise so I can arrange them on the board in a way that will facilitate the later discussion. For example, a simple scheme of this kind would put questions of form in one column and questions of content in another. You could further break this down by grouping questions about particular aspects of form, and by separating questions about the general themes and meanings of the piece from more particular questions about the meanings of individual images and words. If you identify these general groupings before the exercise, you are usefully reminding students of some of the categories they can be thinking about and into which their questions can fall.

VARIATIONS ON QUESCUSSION

Any text or passage, including theoretical and critical writing, can be the subject for a quescussion. Difficult-to-chew bits of gristly theory or richly flavoured chunks of prose make very good subjects.

Quescussion can also work extremely well for debating **issues**. It has proved to be very useful in handling a variety of subjects, notably especially controversial ones, and works across a wide range of class sizes. In large classes, it is particularly useful because it allows a lot of students to make brief contributions without interventions by the professor and because the exercise can be put to several uses.

In this use of quescussion, the statement or subject you give the class (I prefer to offer a challenge via a statement that I may or may not believe rather than just announce a subject) is again crucial. In other disciplines, we could easily imagine a productive quescussion initiated by statements such as "Abortion is a woman's right" or "Better no industry than a polluting industry" or "Genetic engineering is our species's best hope." Similarly, the texts we teach bring up a very wide range of issues, and those issues can provide useful subjects for quescussion.

Less obvious is the option of **using quescussion self-reflexively** to ask questions about the study of poetry. Here again the leading statement or announced subject is crucial since it puts a spin on at least the opening part of the quescussion. These might include such general statements as "Studying poetry provides wide-ranging intellectual benefits and deep pleasures" or "Poetry has never done anything useful in the world," or the more particular "In hip-hop, poetry is returning to its origins in music and musical rhythms."

Essay topics and exam questions can also be useful subjects for class quescussions. They give students training in general and discipline-specific problem-solving skills.

Be creative. What's here is hardly exhaustive, and I'm sure you can come up with variations particularly suited to your teaching situation.

Exercise 8: Brainstorming

8A. BRAINSTORMING

In its most common form, brainstorming is a group technique used to stimulate creative thinking about a problem, an issue, or a course of action. In the simplest variation on this form, a group intensively and informally gathers ideas about approaches or solutions. For the teaching of poetry then, a brainstorming session could work like a quescussion, but without the necessity of framing everything as a question, and a poem, part of one, or an issue or a problem raised by either could be the subject about which the class generates ideas.

Because the group is only throwing out ideas for consideration, risk is relatively low for students, learning is active rather than passive, and many of the benefits of quescussion come into play. You might even follow the quescussion practise of letting participants speak only every Nth time, which, as in quescussion, prevents the more talkative individuals from dominating the class, avoids potentially extended dialogues between two people, thus making the exercise more widely collaborative, and puts pressure on more members of the group to contribute.

Brainstorming enables a lot of people to participate in a relatively short period of time and to respond to each other without your intervention. It also serves a diagnostic function, letting you know at what level or levels your class is engaging with the text, what they do and don't know and understand, and what you need to do to get them to the place you hope they will be. A brainstorming session need take only a few minutes, and its length will of course vary with the size and complexity of the subject you choose and the dynamics of your class. As with quescussion, stop before it gets painful. Brainstorming can be used at any point in a lecture, either in a planned way or in an unplanned way when a crux in meaning or other interesting problem arises.

8B. Baird's Brainstorming

This technique, so called by me because I first saw brainstorming used this way by environmental chemistry professor *extraordinaire* Colin Baird, is extremely useful as a means of reviewing and/or discovering what a class knows and doesn't know about a given subject, introducing them to it, unearthing misconceptions that should be addressed, and organizing a body of material on a subject. It can even help you set the pedagogic agenda for a unit of a course.

Running the exercise

1. As the technique was introduced to me, the instructor announces a subject or an issue to the class. I've seen Baird use it with acid rain and with global warming, I've seen a psychology professor use it with dreams, and I've used it with a piece of poetry, a theory, a genre or form, or a large aspect of poetic analysis like rhythm. The nature of the subject will depend on the level of the course you're

teaching and where you are in that course. There's no point doing this if you suspect your students know nothing at all about the subject, although I've been pleasantly surprised to find out how much my students know about a wide variety of subjects when they pool their knowledge. They've been pleasantly surprised too.

2. The exact task set or challenge offered is crucial. Ask the students for anything they know *or have heard or read* about the subject. Impress upon them that they are not taking ownership of all they say, that anything "out there" is fair game, even if they saw it on the cover of *The National Enquirer* in the supermarket checkout line. For instance, during the brainstorming session on dreams, one contributor said, "I've heard that if you dream you die, you die." This observation got a laugh from some, made a few others look a little puzzled or worried, produced a spike in attention, and was, as outlined in the paragraphs below, recorded on the board without comment by the instructor (although he did hesitate to think about where to place it).

3. The instructor records on the board or the overhead, usually in an abbreviated but intelligible way—this is one of the exercise's challenges for the instructor, and it provides a useful model for students, who learn how to make quick notes and get to see short forms commonly used in the discipline—all the things said, whether they are correct or not. You may comment on things offered, but you need not do so and should keep your comments to a minimum.

4. If possible and desired, the instructor arranges or groups these things in appropriate columns or areas of the board or the overhead. Generally, a board works better here, as it gives you more lateral space for columns or zones. If you're using this technique in a large class, where it works very well but the board doesn't, you'll want to use two overhead projectors. The categories into which the material the class offers will be organized should be planned in advance and will depend on the subject. An obvious schema for poetry is to have a column each for general formal properties and meanings, another one for particular images or effects, and one for anything else. While recording, if you're having a good day and thinking quickly and clearly, you can try to match things in one column with something already there in another, to organize the material on the board

in such a way that spatial connections are made for students. Don't worry if you see connections later that you missed while recording, or if you put the odd thing down in the wrong place. You can always rearrange things or draw arrows or asterisks when you move to the next step.

5. When the class has nothing more to add, or when a time limit has been reached, or there's already more stuff than can possibly be dealt with, the instructor comments on the items. You can do this in a number of ways, depending on how you wish to use the exercise. If it is an introduction and a diagnostic, for instance, you might comment on how much the class already knows about the subject and point out which areas will receive further attention in future sessions. At this point, you should have a pretty good idea of where this class is in relation to the subject. Further, you will know what misconceptions or misinformation the class has about this subject and can begin to correct those early. Since you accepted all the comments uncritically earlier, by the time you deal with the errors they will have been separated in time and in the class's collective memory from the people who made them (and who never claimed ownership of the errors anyway), all of which spares those students public shame and lowers the psychological temperature for participants. If you have grouped the items as suggested above, you might draw attention to your groupings now. I often ask my students if they can figure out the logic of the groupings, at which point the brightest ones sometimes suggest other approaches or categories. When using this method at the introduction of a unit of the course, I also take time at this point to talk about the big picture, to discuss the interrelation of the elements of this subject that we will discuss in future sessions.

6. During the discussion I invite students to comment on the validity and accuracy of the recorded comments. The more critical and analytical work they do, the better they get at it, and the more self-critical (but in a good way) they become. While you have to be very active during this part of the exercise and tie the loose ends together as well as possible, you don't have to do all the work or the debunking of false knowledge or sloppy interpretation.

Exercise 9: The Cumulative Reading

This is another group reading exercise, probably the one I use most often. It focuses on meaning and affect rather than performance, although it can also include considerations of metrical and rhythmic effects and just about anything else. Its strategy is to break a poem or passage into small chunks and assign the chunks serially to individuals or small groups. Students are given some time to think about the form, meaning, figurative language, metre, whatever, in their unit, and are told they will have only one minute (or two) to say as much as they can about their lines when their turn comes. After that, there will be a further two minutes (or three or more depending on the size of the assigned chunks and the size of the class) when the rest of the class can add whatever they want, and then you move on to the next student or group.

The precise way you run the reading will vary with the size and level of the class and with the nature, especially variations in the form, of the piece you are working with. The example I'm using here, if you want to imagine along with the exercise, is the opening eighteen lines of Alexander Pope's *Essay on Man*, partly because this exercise works extremely well with couplets, partly because by training I'm an eighteenth-century specialist and I had to get some of that period's poetry in here, and partly because I tried this passage with a group of non–English specialists at a conference on university teaching and they seemed to enjoy it and feel good about how well they understood it after a mere twenty minutes of communal work. That said, as I'm sure you'll see, the cumulative reading can be used with any piece of poetry (or prose, or film stills, as I've done in film classes) that can be broken down into convenient-sized units such as lines, pairs of lines, stanzas, sentences, verse paragraphs, and so on. Generally, it's best to use the smallest unit that can, more or less, stand on its own, although one of the things that this exercise will demonstrate to the class is how our understandings of meanings and affects are in a process of constant modification and fine tuning as we gather more and more evidence and become aware of a more complex web of interrelations.

Here is the passage, so you have something concrete to focus on while thinking about how this exercise might work:

Know then thyself, presume not God to scan;
The proper study of mankind is Man.
Placed on this isthmus of a middle state,
A being darkly wise, and rudely great:
With too much knowledge for the skeptic side,   5
With too much weakness for the Stoic's pride,
He hangs between; in doubt to act, or rest,
In doubt to deem himself a God, or beast;
In doubt his mind or body to prefer,
Born but to die, and reasoning but to err;   10
Alike in ignorance, his reason such,
Whether he thinks too little, or too much:
Chaos of thought and passion, all confused;
Still by himself abused, or disabused;
Created half to rise, and half to fall;   15
Great lord of all things, yet a prey to all;
Sole judge of truth, in endless error hurled:
The glory, jest, and riddle of the world!
—*From* Alexander Pope, *An Essay on Man*, Epistle II

Running the exercise

1. Put the passage up on an overhead, even if everybody has a text.
Whether the students look up or down, you want the passage in
front of them: it is the focus of the class, not you.
2. Explain the exercise to the class, as described above. Stress that
their response does not have to be, indeed cannot be, exhaustive,
and all they need come up with is a minute or two of material to de-
liver to the class. Tell them how much time they will have to prepare
their material.
3. Break the class into individuals or groups and assign them their
lines. For instance, with the above passage, which has nine couplets,
I'd break a tutorial of twenty into nine groups (seven of two and
two of three), or an honours class of thirty-six into nine groups of
four, and give them five to ten minutes to prepare. That will leave
me about forty minutes: a minute or two for each group to present,
and three or two minutes respectively for the rest of the class to join
in. Time limits should be strictly enforced, because you want to get
everyone involved. When selecting the passage for your class and

trying to work out logistics of group size and allotted time, bear in mind (as I haven't done here) that groups of three tend to stay on task better than groups of two and that larger groups allow individuals within those groups to hide or disappear. I have never run this exercise by assigning units to individuals except once, in a graduate course on heroic couplet poetry when I assigned verse paragraphs of Dryden's *MacFlecknoe* to the students. That worked very well, but for undergraduates the chance to pretest their ideas in their small groups seems to lead to much more productive discussions.

4. For the five to ten minutes that the students are working on their lines, I roam through the class eavesdropping and answering questions (most often by asking other questions). If a group is stuck or needs the meaning of a word, I will provide some help. You needn't do that, but I find that doing so makes the exercise more like what it is, a communal enterprise rather than a test of individuals.

5. Do the cumulative reading. Remind students that, as they move through the passage, they should refer back to what has already been said and make connections between their material and other parts of the piece. You may be pleasantly surprised at how good and thorough a reading you get when all the groups put their observations together and at how excited a class can become over their own discoveries.

6. While this exercise doesn't need unpacking, I like to read the passage at the end. Students then derive much more pleasure from the text precisely because they are more aware of and sensitive to its nuances and fine effects.

Exercise 10: Bring a Question or Statement about the Text

Both of these exercises serve a variety of functions, among them reviewing and diagnosing (an opportunity to locate areas of difficulty and offer help or clarification), highlighting individuals' insights and understandings, fostering independent learning, allowing students to set an agenda for the learning they need, teaching them how to ask productive questions, and getting them to actually read the text before class.

10A. QUESTIONS

This version of the exercise is pretty self-explanatory, works with just about any text, and is especially good for a first-year tutorial (or an upper-level class on a challenging piece of poetry).

Running the exercise
1. Ask students to bring to the next session a question, large or small, about any aspect of the text. I often suggest that they prepare two, in case somebody else asks the same question. If you want to spend a whole lecture or tutorial or a large part of one on this exercise, ask the whole class to bring questions. If you want to spend some fraction of the class period on this exercise, ask an appropriate number of students to bring questions, then work your way through the whole group over a number of sessions.
2. Take up these questions in turn.
3. I try to get the other members of the class to answer the question first; then I return to the questioner, who often has formulated an answer; and only after that do I add whatever else I might have to offer.

10B. STATEMENTS

Although this version of the exercise can be used just as the questions are above, with the statements as the subjects of brief discussions, I prefer to use statements at the end of a discussion of a text or unit of a course, or at the end of the entire course, as a review and summary.

Running the exercise
1. Ask students to bring to the next session something important (it needn't be the most important thing—that makes the exercise too hard—although students usually pick something that means a good deal to them) that they want to say about the subject at hand. It could be something they like or don't like, an insight they've had, something important they've learned, or whatever. Restrict each student to a single sentence.
2. Go around the class in turn.
3. Record the statements on the board or overhead as they are de-

livered. Invite students to comment on or add to each statement, but restrict these observations to one sentence also, or you'll never get through the exercise.

4. As with the questions version above, I add what I think is necessary or useful only after the students have spoken.

5. If you're using the exercise as review and summary, reproduce the comments for distribution to the students. If you're going to use this option, tell students at the beginning of the class so they're not frantically trying to keep their own record of all the comments and thereby making it more difficult for them to participate in the exercise.

Exercise 11: The One-Minute Paper

This widely used technique teaches students to prepare short responses to a question, issue, or text, and it allows for several speakers in a short time. While it was not designed specifically for poetry, it is as useful here as it is elsewhere, and it can be used in a number of ways, including in conjunction with other exercises in this book. For example, Bring a Statement, described just above, is a variation on the One-Minute Paper, with the difference that the former is prepared before class, with more time for reflection, while the latter is done on the spot. Each has its advantages.

Running the exercise

11A. THE ONE-MINUTE PAPER AS A SPRINGBOARD TO DISCUSSION

Students are given a brief period of time (it can be literally one, two, or three minutes but not longer) to write a one-sentence response on what they perceive to be the most important aspect, or merely an important or interesting element of the assigned subject, which can be a text, a problem, an issue, or a question. This can be done individually, or in pairs or threes, and then a number of responses are read aloud to the class, either by the students (the method I prefer) or by you. Because the exercise is limited in time and in the amount students can say, the long speeches that some class members like to give are eliminated, and the responses tend to be more precise. If you don't respond to each individual, a lot of viewpoints can be gathered quickly. One way to follow up on this is to have some of the most useful responses written onto overheads or the board and used as a springboard for further lecturing or discussion. If resources allow, you can even distribute blank overhead slides and pens so that the students can prepare the projections themselves. Privileging those good responses also assigns value to student contributions and encourages students to believe their insights are important.

11B. The One-Minute Paper as an Exit Survey, Diagnostic, or Agenda Setter

End the class with a one-minute paper, as described above, without reading out any responses. Instead, collect them and begin your next class with a summary of what the class has written and your response to that material. Your response can offer any or all of: a review, a correction of misconceptions, a summary of their ideas, a clearing up of problems or issues that have arisen, and a segue to the next part of the course (as you point out which among their observations will come into play for the next text).

11C. The Cumulative Reading as a One-Minute Exercise

In this variation of Exercise 9 above, rather than assigning specific lines to individuals or groups, divide a task or problem into several parts and assign those parts to various zones or fractions of the class. For instance, you might ask some groups to deal with figurative language in assigned stanzas, others to scan particular lines, others to deal with tone or rhythm or punctuation or whatever. Give them a brief period to work up an answer, with the instruction that their answer need not be comprehensive and cannot take more than a minute. Call for one or more responses from a class fraction. After one or more people have spoken for a minute on their part of the problem, other members of that group can add supplementary information. Then move on to the next group until all fractions have been represented. As noted above, this variation can work with the analysis of all kinds of texts, including theoretical, critical, and literary texts, with slides and film stills, and with various kinds of problems and issues.

Exercise 12: Group Role-Playing or Mass Debate

This exercise pits one large section of the class in debate/discussion with one or more other fractions of the class. It can be a very liberating way to encourage broad interaction and participation, especially in a large class where sheer size acts as a disincentive to participation. The instructor assigns appropriate opposing positions to parts of the class regardless of what side of the issue students would choose to take. For the teaching of poetry, these opposing sides could find their origins in an issue or a problem in an individual poem or the context to which the poem is responding (say, Milton's Satan as hero or villain in *Paradise Lost*, or Eliot's view of culture in *The Waste Land*) or in setting two poems that offer radically different points of view against one another (say, nature in Pope's *Windsor Forest* versus Wordsworth's in *Tintern Abbey* or James Thomson's in *The Seasons*). Naturally, these oppositions will vary with the specific course and material that you're teaching, but they may be political, ideological, theoretical, moral, ethical, or otherwise philosophical, methodological, interpretive, and so on. In a large class dealing with a complex issue, you can, of course, use more than two positions for the class to model.

Running the exercise

1. In the session before the one in which you run the exercise, announce the subject or topic that is to be treated and introduce the problem in appropriate detail. At that time, you can assign roles so students can think about a particular side of the controversy or issue, or you can ask them to think generally about all sides of the issue without assigning specific roles. Point out where they can do some relevant reading.

2. The debate or discussion seems to work best when the various positions are defined in quite polar terms. Asked to take extreme positions, students will less likely feel that they could be mistaken as representing their own positions, attitudes, and understandings.

3. The instructor begins by setting out the question or issue for debate in whatever detail is required, and then acts as moderator. Once the thing gets going, stand back a little. Don't respond to what the speakers say; let them speak to and challenge one another.

Your role is partly that of the speaker of the house, identifying the next to speak and loosely monitoring behaviour, and partly as a guide, intervening briefly, occasionally, and strategically to keep the discussion along profitable lines without stifling some of the levity that almost always comes with this exercise.

4. This type of discussion can run for quite a while and has its own energy. It's dangerous to run since it relies on heavy student input and goodwill, you have to be deft on your feet to steer the thing a little from time to time, and doing the debriefing that should follow the mass debate requires agility too. But a bit of danger can spice up your teaching and raise your energy level, and there always seem to be enough people who like to speak in a large group.

Exercise 13: The Shape of Poems

Poetry is spatial

Whether the poetry is the most traditional and rigidly formal, free verse, or emblem or concrete, the spatial arrangement of phonemes, words, lines, stanzas or other formal units, and the whole poem on the page is as much in a good poet's and good reader's mind as are the rhythmic and sonic elements of the poem to which they are deeply bound. While several of the exercises above try to find a way into poetry by means of its aural qualities, emphasizing poetry's more public and performative aspects, tapping into its specifically spatial and visual qualities is also important. The pleasures that the ordering and disordering or rhythms and sounds bring to the material and the mind's ear are here matched by pleasures delivered by the real and the inner eye, and by the pleasure we find in the spatial arrangement of things, whether it be a picturesque or sublime landscape, the shape of one we love, or the well-wrought poem on the page. Clearly, this sense of poetry is worth developing.

For many of us, a fundamental link exists between space, including the space within which things happen, and the memory of the things that happened in that space. Often, when I try to recall something that happened or something I have read, what will swim into consciousness just before or alongside the memory is the site of the event or the place on the page. This was brought home to me powerfully when I was teaching *Rape of the Lock* one year, and I had introduced the class to the term *oxymoron* and written it on the board in my usual attempt to preempt creative spellings. (I once got an exam answer on *Paradise Lost* that told me quite a bit about Satin and the Fallen Angles; there are pleasures here too, but I don't think so well of myself for feeling them. They smack too much of schadenfreude.) When in the next session I was talking about another oxymoron in the poem, I pointed to the now blank spot on the board where I had written the word the previous day. About a third of my class nodded or smiled, and when I asked a few of them about it, they noted that focussing on that space had brought to mind the term's meaning. Memories and their spaces, for at least some of my students and for me, seem to be stored together. Similarly, an important part of what makes poetry memorable and pleasing is the way it arranges space both within its own lines and on the page.

I find this sense of the architectonics of poetry and the pleasures that derive from it difficult to instil in all but a few of my students. I suspect many of my students find it frustrating to witness me demonstrating and enthusing about a sense and pleasure they have difficulty sharing. Nevertheless, I continue to try, and to not be content, as Milton pretended to be, with reaching "the fit, though few." Here are some things I've tried.

13A. MARKING UP A TEXT ON THE BOARD OR OVERHEAD

We graphically chart connections and relations among ideas, phrases, clauses, images, words, and sounds when preparing for classes or doing our own reading, but our beginning students generally don't know how to do this. We should both demonstrate the technique and give students practise in class by collectively mapping connections using an appropriate scheme of underlining, circling, drawing arrows, using coloured markers, and so on. I usually prepare at least one overhead showing a page from one of my teaching texts, which are all heavily marked up in preparation for classes. Teaching students to mark up a text not only highlights spatial relations in the piece (obviously, you can do this with prose as well), but also helps them get over the panic or anxiety of trying to understand the whole poem at once. I write a few lines on the board (it's easier to change things as you go along; having coloured chalk helps), then turn them into an exercise involving the whole class. Alternatively, you can run this exercise using Think, Pair, Share, as described below. I regularly use this wonderful "a plague on both their houses" couplet from Pope's *Moral Essays*, "Epistle II: Of the Characters of Women":

A Fop their Passion, but their Prize a Sot,
Alive, ridiculous, and dead, forgot!   (lines 247–48)

This couplet proves particularly useful because its meaning is not so readily available to most of my students until they have worked through and marked up the couplet, and in many cases until they have learned the meanings of "Fop" and "Sot" (I supply dictionary definitions here, as I do for Negotiating a Group Reading above, to encourage students to use good dictionaries regularly). By the time they've marked up the passage, students are usually pleasantly surprised to see that they now fill in the elisions (which themselves say something about the ideology and use of space in the poem), understand this somewhat cryptic passage, and gain confidence in their developing ability to analyse and understand what was at first opaque.

13B. LOOKING AT SPATIAL ELEMENTS IN THE BROADER, FORMAL,
AND MATERIAL QUALITIES OF POETRY

Before I employ this method of highlighting spatial qualities in poetry, I usually wait until students have studied or at least encountered a variety of poetic forms (e.g., the sonnet, the ode, the heroic couplet, and so on) from various periods or through the more detailed examination of a single period. This exercise usually begins by showing students, on overhead slides or, if the class is small enough, within period volumes or facsimiles, how different types of poetry appear on the page. Through its use of space, for example, a royal quarto edition of late eighteenth-century lyric poetry showing the proverbial rivulet of text meandering through a meadow of margin says something about that poetry and reveals at least some of that age's or writer's ideology. So does an emblem poem, an ode or particular type of sonnet of the seventeenth century, a heroic-couplet poem of the eighteenth, a concrete poem of the twentieth, or an e.e. cummings or bp nichol or bill bissett poem that eschews capitalization. Comparing the appearance of a single poem in editions from various periods, and what those appearances signify—including, of course, the version in students' own anthologies—can be an interesting exercise in itself. In doing such exercises, it is often difficult, even impossible, to disentangle the spatial from the formal and material qualities of a poem on the page, but that is something worth pointing out and discussing also.

13C. MINING A SINGLE VISUAL OR SPATIAL ELEMENT OF A POEM FOR ITS SIGNIFICATAIONS

In my eightenth-century courses, I usually spend a class on the architectonics and dominant patterns of the heroic couplet. In a theory class in which I was introducing de Saussure, signs, signifiers, and so on to second-year students, I used the example of the dash in an Emily Dickinson poem, exploring with the class the various meanings and uses of the dash, including how it affected space and the interrelations of spaces in the poem.

*

Designing Your Own Exercises

Principles to bear in mind when devising exercises are:

- The task and issue have to be very clearly defined. Vague questions and unclear procedures are deadly.
- Students have to feel safe to participate freely, to be able to take reasonable risks with what they say.
- Remember that you don't have to respond to everything every student says. Often, one objective of these exercises is to get maximum participation and interaction among students in a short time. If they can't all talk to you and the class at large, at least they can talk to each other.
- To that end, you might incorporate into your exercises, or employ on its own, a widely used technique commonly called Think, Pair, Share. Despite its saccharine title, this technique has real merit and is incorporated into some of the exercises above. It works like this:

Think, Pair, Share and Beyond

- A clearly defined task to be done for a short, specified time period is assigned to class members.

- To start off, students are asked to think for a minute or so on their own, and then to exchange their thoughts with one or two other class members for a further two or three minutes. In general, groups of three are more likely to stay on task than are pairs.
- After this initial discussion and the preparation of a response or statement by the group, the instructor can call for the responses to be delivered to the class, or can ask each group to join two or three other groups (how large these can get will depend in part on the configuration of the room in which you are teaching and the size of your class) to exchange, compare, and summarize responses.
- This step can be repeated until groups reach maximum workable size, and then the groups report to the whole class. Overheads or the board can be used at this point to record responses.
- Another way to configure this exercise is to do it twice: once at the beginning of the class, where pairs or triads of students give each other their first takes on an issue or subject, and then again after a lecture or other form of instruction on that subject. These responses don't always have to be communicated to the whole class.

*

A Few Concluding Aphorisms
and Thoughts

I'm not teaching if no one is learning.

Different students have different learning styles; variety is useful for a lot of reasons.

Decentralizing the teacher can centre students and texts.

By no means am I advocating that we give our classes over entirely to such exercises as those described here. Although we have to be much more than mere conveyers of data, which oral transmission to an audience of mixed interests and abilities dooms to sometimes sad and sometimes funny imperfection anyway, our pedagogy retains (and remains) a very important place for lecturing, for the many important types of content that we traditionally provide, and for the example we provide of someone enthusiastic and knowledgeable doing the work and experiencing the pleasure of the discipline.

Taking chances by relying on the more or less unpredictable contributions of others can lead to the best and most exciting classes. It can, of course, also lead to the worst and most embarrassing. What I mean by taking chances in this specific context is in devising classes that use student participation to achieve course objectives. It can take imagination and daring to design and execute the discipline-specific exercises to do that, but the payoff is large for the instructor and the students.

I continue to try to find ways to open wider for myself and for my students the magic casements of poetry, always believing that what I did last week was my juvenilia and that this week or next I will do better. If what you have read here helps you on your own quest to more effective teaching, or better yet to devising strategies that work well for you and your students, I will be very happy indeed. If you tell me about your discoveries (agedalof@uwo.ca), I'll be happier still, and if a further edition of this handbook is ever called for, I will incorporate and fully acknowledge those useful materials I receive. As students and teachers of literature, we work hard to communicate to one another, through conferences and publications, the things we have uncovered or discovered about our subject material, but we do little to share with one another the things we have learned about how to teach that material to our students. As always, we could do better.

The truths and beauties of great literature, provisional as they always are, still outlast and will outlast the truths and beauties of great science. What we do matters a great deal. If we don't believe that, we shouldn't be doing it.

Index